Still Not at Ease

By Laura Hewett

Illustrations by Tessa Sydnor

Ger-bear, I'll pray for you when the alarm goes off today.

Amanda, I'll make an effort to love well today.

Carol, I'll take care of myself responsibly today.

Nathan, I'll listen to others carefully today.

Tessa, I'll create something new in hopes of inspiring today.

Preface

The spring - and summer and fall and winter - of 2020 was weird for all of us. In the first lockdown, I watched particular hardship in two different people very close to me that caused me a lot of grief and confusion which eventually led me to write my first poem that summer. Within weeks, my own life had profound events that left me at a loss for prose to make sense of it. I began writing poetry almost constantly late summer and through the fall and winter to try and capture the layers I was living. Tessa asked to illustrate some of my poems to share in a collection, and I'm honored to have my words next to her art. The title of this collection comes from a line of poetry by one of my students who journeyed beside me through some of my strange summer. Our overlapping experience birthed this beautiful stanza in her poem titled "The Summer of Trees."

This year had a summer of trees
A summer of cheesecake and bees
When the river came fast
I thought "We won't last!"
But we did, and I'm still not at ease
                   by Felicity Miller

Contents

The Princess Tree

Blessed is the one
who is planted by
streams of water

Made for the island
some seeds were stolen
planted in darkness

Meant to be more
celebrating life and growth
Symbol of Unity

Rerooted in the forest
you were landlocked instead
still growing tall

Where others meant harm
your roots grew deep
as nature intended

When were you infected?
What did they do?
Innocence was lost.

It's not your fault
you can be redeemed
seasons are changing

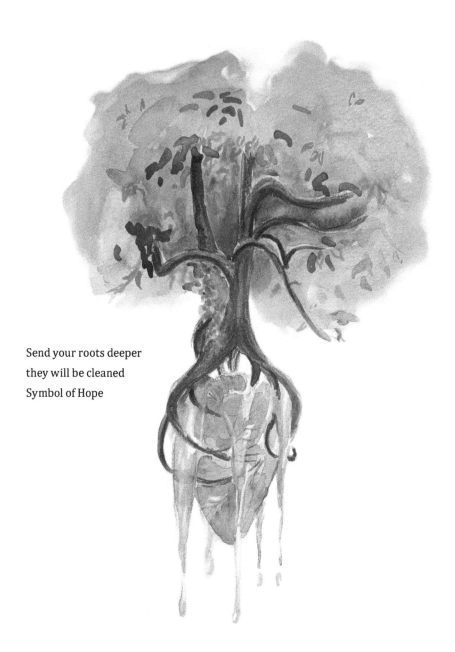

Send your roots deeper
they will be cleaned
Symbol of Hope

Grafted In

I'm a branch of a tree.
Grown from one place
Grafted to another

I'm part of a bigger story.
Written all alone
Revised as a member

I'm living beyond my limited means.
Birthed as an outsider
Brought into a family

I'm able to give good fruit.
Moved from a poisoned root
Motivated to share

Heart of Flesh

The tree was green this morning
It's yellow tonight
Leaves mottled with brown
The seasons change

My heart was stone this morning
It's beating tonight
I see hurting people around
Vulnerability bleeds me

The tree wasn't made to stagnate
New leaves will grow
Shedding old leaves is part of life
Spring returns again

I'm supposed to breathe
Steady heart beat
I'm not made of metal or stone
I'll sing again

Of Trees and Trials

This would be easier if I were a tree
Planted in the ground, growing tall

I wouldn't have to worry about emotions if I were a tree
Leaves rustling in the wind, changing colors

My heart wouldn't hurt if I were a tree
Roots growing deeper, finding nourishment

I could declare goodness and creativity
Displaying splendor in season, according to its kind

Instead I'm a human
Moving from place to place, representing love

I've been hurt on this journey
Just like them all, learning empathy

I've learned obedience to something bigger
Others can see my healing, loving generously

My story is different than what I wanted to write
It has more colors and growth, according to its kind

Autumn Leaf

The leaf turns from green
To crimson velveteen

She curls up to dry
While I display her inside

Born outside in spring
She still has joy to bring

There's meaning in a single leaf
According to my belief

God cares for my single soul

The Name of the Drizzle

When a tropical storm becomes a hurricane
They give it a name.

When I woke up on Tuesday
There was a drizzle.

No one noticed the difference
But I called it by Name.

When the weather changes
I notice God move.

When the ground dries out
The Spirit still breathes in the leaves.

The River

Flow down
Run free
Wash me clean

Cold source
Rushing flow
It isn't easy

Dirty current
Holy water
Different than appearances

Winding water
Twisting turns
Full of surprises

Don't quench
River, come
I will persevere

The Oasis

It's hot out here.
It's dry too.
I'm parched.

The desert sand extends every direction.
There's no respite or mountain in sight.
I hear rumbling.

Not a cloud is in the sky.
No breeze has come for years.
I'm going to die in this desert.

Did you blink?

I hear the sound of water rushing
I hear thunder breaking too.
Was that a flash of lightening?

I didn't think it was possible.
I don't understand.
Is the ground wet with raindrops?

I think this is more than a shower.
I think a flood is coming.
Hey, is that roaring sound water?

It stayed even after I blinked again.

That mountain wasn't there before.
The glacier is new too.
I think something big is happening.

There's a river coming from the oasis.
The oasis is new too.
I'm probably dreaming.

This is too good to be true.
This isn't a story I could imagine.
I'm going to be rescued.

The Wrestling Match

I was told to meet you here in the event room;
There was a challenge.

Instead of a wrestling mat I found a dance floor;
This is an invitation.

My story shifted when I took your hand;
There is no fight as you direct me.

I don't lose agency when I trust your lead;
You respond when I lean in.

The dance progresses when we move in circles;
What looks like the same place has covered more ground.

You spin me out;
I hold on tightly knowing I come back to you.

You keep me safe;
We advance a conversation with our whole beings.

Robot in a Convent

The world outside has so much space
The world inside is ordered and clean
The little robot confines herself

The people outside have so much love
The people inside keep quiet and hide
The little robot is scared of love

The colors outside have such vibrancy
The colors inside are muted and dull
The little robot doesn't see the rainbows

The air outside is fresh and moves
The air inside is stale and still
The little robot forgets she has lungs

The life outside invites community
The life inside rejects relationship
The little robot was made to be a human

What If

What if I was right all along?
What if you do love me?

What if I'm gifted and strong?
What if you care for me?

Would my world be different
If I live in that identity?

What if I thrive and win?
What if that's what you wanted for me?

What if I share and teach?
What if that's what you created for me?

Would the world be a better place
If I embrace my identity?

Identity

Who did I see in the mirror every day for the past year?
She wasn't there today.

Who did I see when I was seven?
Did I see a glimmer of her joy just now?

Who did I see when I was sixteen?
Did I catch a glimpse of her hope this morning?

Who did I see when I was twenty-four?
Did I recognize her growing confidence in passing?

Who did I see when I was thirty?
Did I notice her grace today?

Who is this woman in the mirror now?
There's something new I see that's always been me.

Known

I don't know you
Can you tell me about yourself?

I want to be known
I don't want to share anything with you.

You don't know me
Would you be careful with these details about me?

Don't expect me to know you
We've never spoken before today.

There's more to know
Would you like to have a conversation?

I don't know

Look to the Skies

Open your eyes
I know it's terrifying
It's still worth trying

Open your eyes
Face down all the fear
I'm standing with you here

Open your eyes
There's space to move
You have nothing to prove

Open your eyes
Look to the skies

Open your eyes
Look to the skies

Look to the skies
Where anxiety dies
Open your heart to new things

Look to the skies
Unlearn the lies
Embrace the truth of your identity

Look to the skies
It's not about tries
This moment was made for action

Look to the skies
Open your eyes
Step into peace

Encounter

Open your eyes
Look to the skies
The Lord is moving

Hear the leaves
Listen to the trees
The Spirit is speaking

Stand in the rain
Feel someone else's pain
Jesus is healing

I See Stars

Deep in the woods
When you look to the sky
You only see darkness

Out in the streets
There's space in between
You can witness the galaxy

This is the place
Familiar in my memory
You sprinkled stars generously

Back in the forest
Nature connections expected
You blind yourself in density

Open spaces await
Where vulnerability is exposed
You recognize that intimacy

Come to the table
Be welcomed home lovingly
You can see the stars too

The Seasons of Your Voice

In the summer there was surety
I recognized your call
I'd heard echoes through all spring

In the autumn words came subtly
I trusted as leaves fall
I'd lost confidence in what you'd bring

In the winter I yelled angrily
I couldn't hear your call
I'd been left with a deep hungering

In the spring I slept peacefully
I chose faith that wouldn't fall
I'd found peace beyond understanding

Call to Prayer

There's so much sickness in the world.

Can you hear the Bells?

Let's pray.

There's so much hurt in the world.

Can you hear the Bells?

Let's pray.

There's so much hate in the world.

Can you hear the Bells?

Let's pray.

There's so much confusion in the world.

Can you hear the Bells?

Let's pray.

It doesn't have to be this way.

I want to add clarity to the world.

Can you hear the Bells?

Let's pray.

I want to add love to the world.
Can you hear the Bells?
Let's pray.

I want to add comfort to the world.
Can you hear the Bells?
Let's pray.

I want to add healing to the world.
Can you hear the Bells?
Let's pray.

Break the Dam

Fear has no place here.

Break it down.

Replace it with the rushing peace of your refreshing comfort.

Doubt has no place here.

Break it down.

Replace it with roaring assurance of your absolute confidence.

Hate has no place here.

Break it down.

Replace it with raging floods of your overwhelming love.

Anger has no place here.

Break it down.

Replace it with refreshing waves of your calming patience.

Desperation has no place here.

Break it down.

Replace it with reassuring streams of your righteous passion.

Fury and chaos have no place here.

Break it down.

Replace it with Rest.

Naaman's Prayer

The Israeli servant said,
Go to the prophet of YHWH.
There is a God who hears
who speaks
who heals.

I said,
Here are the prophets of Rimmon.
They have no ears
no voice
no power.

The prophet Elisha said,
Go to the Jordan River.
The LORD of Israel will make you clean.

I said,
Here I am of Syria.
Don't I have better rivers
armies
friends?

My servants said,
We've come so far.
Will your pride keep you from washing
from victory
from community?

The LORD spoke;
He met me in the river.
He washed me clean of pride
of ignorance
oh, and leprosy.

Prayer for a Mini-Me

Lord, you showed up in fire when I asked you to.
Lord, you showed up in wind when I was alone.
Lord, you sent me to care for this little one.

This little one you gave me is more than I can handle.
He has way more resources than I do.
How can I be any help to him?

This little one you gave me just wants to learn from me.
He has way more capacity for understanding than I do.
How can I be any help to him?

This little one you gave me asked to hear your voice like I do.
He has way more ability to act on your word than I do.
How can I be any help to him?

This little on you gave me wants to integrate his faith and life more fully.
He has more drive to articulate that unity than I do.
How can I be any help to him?

This little one you gave me feels the tension in the love he has for friends who turn
away from you.
He has far more reach than I ever could.
How can I be any help to him?

This little one you gave me isn't ready to be on his own.
He told me he's scared.
I've been scared before.
I know I can help him.

This little one you gave me cried when I said I would die someday.
He told me to shut up.
I've been quiet before.
I know I can help him.

This little one you gave me is going to do greater things than I can imagine.
He can soar with the eagles.
I'll teach him to fly.
I know I can help him.

Lord, open his eyes to see the fire.
Lord, open his ears to hear the wind.
Lord, send him to the masses beyond what I can reach.

Bless Me

My father,
My grandfather,
My grandfather's concubine
They said Your Name after encounters with different aspects of you:
The God who Sees, who Provides, who Is Faithful
Bless me

My brother didn't understand what he gave me
I didn't understand what I stole
But I wanted more of you
Bless me

My uncle didn't know you but he could recognize you at work
He gave me love and money
But I wanted more
Bless me

Children are a joy and they multiply in my home like sheep
A nation comes from me
Who will they be
Bless me

All this good from the worldly things isn't enough
I want to encounter you
Bless me

"Blessed to be a blessing"
You promised that before
This abundance isn't enough
I want to share more
Bless me

I'll fight you here, but not just for me
The wrestling match is an invitation
I won't let go tonight until you
Bless me

The story starts where I thought it would end
The sun comes up and I'm limping again
I won't forget how you continue to
Bless me

I won't settle for less than intimacy
With a God who gives over abundantly
Now that I've seen that I'm ready to share how you
Bless me

It looks different than before
Because you actually love me more
You taught me generosity when you
Bless me

I'm still in brokenness
And you don't love someone less
When I demand you
Bless me

There's space for the world to thrive
We don't have to barely survive
I can keep seeking you
LORD, bless me

Untitled

I'm not inadequate

But I can't walk yet

I get flustered when on the spot

For my reconciliation

Is a high priority

Prayer for the Prodigal Son

I love you.
You don't have to run.

The world lied to you.
The world said it was fun.

I love you.
You don't have to hide.

The enemy tricked you.
The enemy put doubt inside.

I love you.
You don't have to cry.

The deceiver wants to hold you back.
The deceiver wants your insides to die.

I love you.
You don't have to hurt.

The monster wants to break you.
The monster shoves your face in the dirt.

I love you.
You can come back.

Your father will always welcome.
Your father will help you unpack.

I love you.
You will be forgiven.

Your mother will open her arms.
Your mother will offer you heaven.

I love you.
You can still grow.

Your brother is waiting for you.
Your brother will share what you know.

I love you.
You will be redeemed.

Your Savior already made payment.
Your Savior is ready and you are seen.

For Vision

The mist clears
The fog remains

The sun is high
The clouds cover the sky

I know it's morning
I wake up with confidence

The dark outside
Doesn't block my way

I still see
I have light

Street lamps and torches
Twinkle in the dusk

Light shines in the darkness
And the darkness has not overcome it

For Freedom

Brick and mortar block the way
Stone and cement seal up the path
The tower is high
The fortress is thick

You don't feel worth the effort
You don't expect to be saved
I was called to smash the strongholds
I was instructed to set you free

This isn't about you
This is bigger than me
Where the Spirit of the Lord is

I'll smash your box of theology
You'll bend my understanding of reality
There is freedom

For Action

I was told not to move
This isn't a game
You're supposed to go first
You get the fame

I saw the picture
Of you with bare feet
You're covering your eyes
Step into peace

I smashed all the strongholds
Chains fell away
You have vision and freedom
And don't have to stay

I can't force your hand
Speaking in abstraction
You won't be manipulated
Into any action

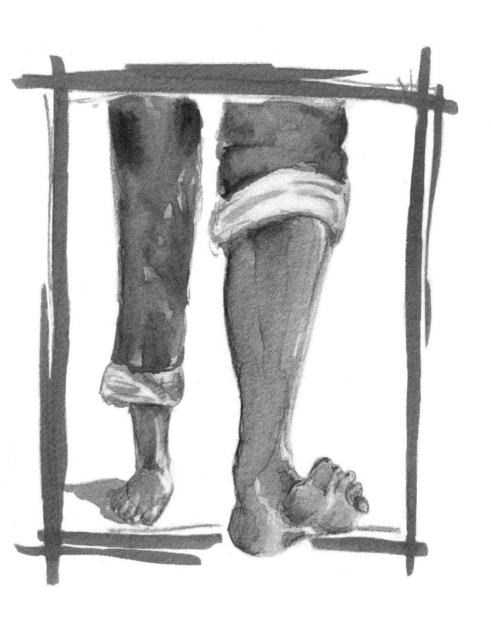

Love and Dust

[To be read aloud on a warm summer evening or a cold winter morning depending on your hemisphere when late June finds you.]

In the beginning there was chaos - until Love spoke light into darkness, separating the waters above from the waters below

And the chaos moved into order
The patterns appeared with complexity and color

Hurt cracked the surface in the harsh sunlight, but the stars sent dust across the crust
Love breathes the dust; dust breathes the love

Science says we're but dust; poetry says we're but love
Truth stitches the two together

Lies rip relationships apart: disorder
Good News recognizes the reality of the brokenness and enters in: reorder can begin

In the middle there is a mess - until Love speaks again, incarnating life among the dust

And dust remembered life comes with love
The wounds don't disappear, but they begin to heal

Night and Dawn come before Day, The Accident
Writers will ponder the words One Generation After

Other voices will listen but not always hear correctly
Someone will twist the truth, but more will hear The Message:

In the end there will be reconciliation - when Love restores and rewards 'according to its kind'

And dry bones will be revived listening to their first Love
Scars will remain to tell the story of redemption

They will tell this story: All shall be well, all shall be well, and in all manner of thing, all shall be well
Hope will pair with Love when the healing comes, but it will never be forced

Will you speak or will you hear:
'Thy will be done'

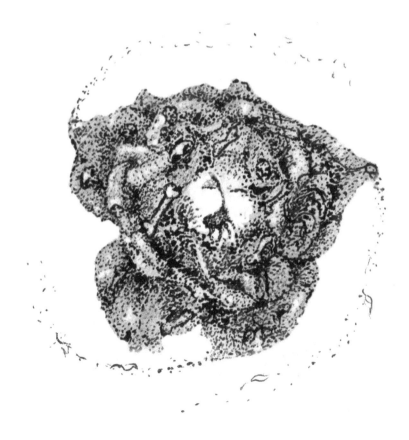

Imago Dei

Male and Female, God created us.

I don't want to be like you.
I don't want you to be like me.

I want to learn from you.
I want you to learn from me.

I think I can sharpen you.
I think you can soften me.

I think I can open your eyes.
I think you can help me grow.

In the Image of God, we were created.

We don't have to shout.
We don't have to hurt.

We can work together.
We can be a team.

We have the capacity to learn.
We have the capacity to grow.

We will be agents of healing.
We will image our God.

Anger at Sunset

You said something wrong
I reacted poorly
The sun moves to mid morning

You refused to repent
I don't have good words
The sun moves to mid afternoon

You don't show signs of growing
I harbor hurt
The sun moves to mid evening

You aren't a perfect person
I'm also a mess
The sun sets

You are still a mess but want to grow
I found a way to tell you I want to reconcile
The sun moves to early morning

Light Up the Sky

The hills are dark.

The clouds are thick.

The lightning strikes.

The sky and trees separate.

The heavens above and the earth below.

The thunder rolls.

The world falls silent.

The sky returns to black.

The rain connects us.

One Point of Light

It might be a star
It might be a satellite
It shows up first and brightest each night

Twinkling in the dusk
Shining in the dark
Holding steady and strong overhead

The clouds try to cover it
The storms try to hide it
The weather can't overcome it

The light is not dependant on me seeing it
Its existence isn't hampered by my acknowledgement
Its glory is not connected to me

A point of light alone in the sky

Tell Me Everything

I want to know it all

Always

I want to see how things fit together

Connect

I want to understand

Complexity

I want to learn about the purpose

Design

I want to find the patterns hidden in details

Growing

I want to know everything

Intimately

Patience

Pray for me
I'm starting to bleed
I'm letting everyone down

My mother doesn't think I'm caring enough
My daughter doesn't come to me for comfort
I need your patience
I'm learning compassion

Pray for me
I'm running so weary
I'm a disappointment to all

My father says I'm not doing enough
My sons ask me for too much attention
I need your patience
I'm learning my identity

Pray for me
I'm not finished yet
I'm not responsible for this mess

My God made me loved as I am
My Lord gifted me sufficiently
I need your patience
I'm learning patience

Give Thanks

If I don't give God glory for the little things
It'll feel foreign to experience the unimaginable

If I live in expectation of the miraculous
It'll be awesome to watch the earth shake

If I know God moves mountains
It'll be a comfort to see the trees sway

If I have faith in the resurrection
It'll seem possible to see reconciliation

If I'm not anticipating blessing
It'll feel uncomfortable to receive gifts

If I'm loved by the God of the universe
It'll be right to constantly give thanks

Resurrection Faith

When Abraham went up the mountain
He expected to return
He expected Isaac to return
He didn't know the details

Did the promise of resurrection make it any easier
To carry the sticks
To build the altar
To sacrifice his son?

The ram caught in the thicket was a plot twist only God knew
The one who provides
The one who plans
The one who knows me intimately

Jesus showed up on the same mountain generations later
To lift himself up
To sacrifice his life
To provide for me

Did the promise of resurrection make it any easier
Being abandoned by his friends
Being beaten and mocked
Being the perfect lamb?

When Jesus rose from the dead he left a promise
Of his provision
Of completion of his work in me
Of my future resurrection

Acknowledgements

Morgan Auten Smith, thank you for a cover design that fits my heart so well.

Chris Bryan, thank you for using your expertise to put together the final details of this process that I don't understand.

Dr. Schaak and Dr. Pothen, I am your firstfruits, and this is my firstfruit. I take that seriously; I hope you're proud.

About the Author

Laura is a friend, a sister,
a daughter, a teacher, a mentor,
a book enthusiast, a theologian, a writer,
an adventurer, a missionary,
and a Jesus lover.